The Passion Play

Leader Guide

THE PASSION PLAY
Living the Story of Christ's Last Days

The Passion Play
978-1-5018-8441-2
978-1-5018-8442-9 eBook

The Passion Play Leader Guide
978-1-5018-8450-4
978-1-5018-8451-1 eBook

The Passion Play DVD
978-1-5018-8443-6

LEADER GUIDE

THE PASSION PLAY

Living the Story of Christ's Last Days

Rob Fuquay

Mike S. Poteet, Contributor

Abingdon Press / Nashville

THE PASSION PLAY
LIVING THE STORY OF CHRIST'S LAST DAYS
LEADER GUIDE

ISBN 13: 978-1-5018-8450-4

19 20 21 22 23 24 25 26 27 28 — 10 9 8 7 6 5 4 3 2 1
MANUFACTURED IN THE UNITED STATES OF AMERICA

CONTENTS

Introduction 7

1. The Power of a Vow 11

2. The Importance of Community 21

3. The Role of Ritual 31

4. Living the Story 39

5. Telling a Better Story 47

6. The Power of the Cross. 57

INTRODUCTION

The decennial (once a decade) Passion Play performed in the Bavarian village of Oberammergau is one of the most famous dramatic productions in the world. As author Rob Fuquay writes in his book *The Passion Play*, "In 2010, more than a half-million people descended upon Oberammergau to attend one of the 102 performances that occurred between May and October. Estimates are even higher for the next production in 2020."

What accounts for the passion play's fame and ability to draw audiences from around the world? Surely its unusual history as one community's ambitious, ongoing fulfillment of a centuries-old vow accounts for much of its renown. But as Fuquay suggests in his book, the play's power also resides in its subject matter, and in its ability to invite us to consider what defines us.

In this six-session study, you and your group will study Fuquay's book together and consider what the Oberammergau passion play can teach Christians about how the Passion of Jesus Christ defines those who believe in and strive to follow him.

In **Session 1, "The Power of a Vow,"** participants will consider the ways vows, oaths, and promises have shaped and continue to shape their lives, as the promise made in Oberammergau in 1634 to mount a passion play every decade continues to shape that community's life and identity.

In **Session 2, "The Importance of Community,"** participants will reflect on communities that have formed (and are still forming) and will identify key characteristics of Christian community with reference to the various ways the Passion Play experience binds together the community of Oberammergau.

In **Session 3, "The Role of Ritual,"** participants will explore the place and power of ritual in their own lives and in the lives of their faith communities, comparing and contrasting their experiences with the experiences of those who live with the rituals surrounding the Oberammergau passion play.

In **Session 4, "Living the Story,"** participants will reflect on what it means to live righteously, looking at the expectations placed on performers in Oberammergau in light of the standards to which Jesus holds his followers.

In **Session 5, "Telling a Better Story,"** participants will confront the ugly legacy of anti-Semitism and anti-Judaism in the way Christians have often told the story of Jesus' passion, and will explore ways to tell the story that better reflect not only Jesus' Jewish identity but also the far-reaching and inclusive love of God.

Finally, in **Session 6, "The Power of the Cross,"** participants will examine one of the Christian faith's most important symbols, and will explore how it has been interpreted in the past and what it means for them and their congregations today.

Suggested Leader Preparation

Before each session:

- Carefully read the chapter of *The Passion Play* being covered in the session, making notes on its main ideas as well as any topics covered or questions raised that especially interest, intrigue, or challenge you.
- Preview the DVD segment for the session, and make arrangements to watch each segment as part of the session. Double-check your audio and visual connections before your session begins!
- Prayerfully read and reflect on each session's Scriptural

Foundation. Mark or write down words, phrases, and images that attract your attention. List the insights and questions you have after reading each passage. Consult trusted Bible commentaries for background information.

- Prepare a comfortable meeting space for your group, accessible to all participants regardless of physical ability. *Optional:* Provide name tags and light refreshments.
- Have markers and a marker board or large sheets of paper available for writing participants' responses.
- Make Bibles available for participants who don't bring their own. *Optional:* Provide trusted Bible dictionaries and commentaries.
- Choose the discussion questions and activities you will use with your group. Gather any additional supplies the activities call for.

May your group's study of the Oberammergau passion play not only increase your awareness and appreciation of this village's unique gift to world culture, but also deepen your faith in him whose story the passion play tells, and strengthen your commitment to live as his faithful disciples!

Session 1

THE POWER OF A VOW

Session Goals

This session's readings, video, conversations, and activities will help participants:

- Explain the origins of the Oberammergau Passion Play tradition.
- Identify how vows have shaped their lives and identities.
- Examine selected biblical vows for insight about how making and keeping vows can help us grow in faith.
- Consider a specific vow they can make to God.

Scriptural Foundation

Jacob left Beer-sheba and set out for Haran. He reached a certain place and spent the night there. When the sun had set, he took one of the stones at that place and put it near his head. Then he lay down there. He dreamed and saw a raised staircase, its foundation on earth and its top touching the sky, and God's messengers were ascending and descending on it. Suddenly the LORD was standing on it and saying, "I am the LORD, the God of your father Abraham and the God of Isaac. I will give you and your descendants the land on which you are lying. Your descendants will become like the dust of the earth; you will spread out to the west, east, north, and south. Every family of earth will be blessed because of you and your descendants. I am with you now, I will protect you everywhere you go, and I will bring you back to this land. I will not leave you until I have done everything that I have promised you."

When Jacob woke from his sleep, he thought to himself, The LORD is definitely in this place, but I didn't know it. He was terrified and thought, This sacred place is awesome. It's none other than God's house and the entrance to heaven. After Jacob got up early in the morning, he took the stone that he had put near his head, set it up as a sacred pillar, and poured oil on the top of it. He named that sacred place Bethel, though Luz was the city's original name. Jacob made a solemn promise: "If God is with me and protects me on this trip I'm taking, and gives me bread to eat and clothes to wear, and I return safely to my father's household, then the LORD will be my God. This stone that I've set up as a sacred pillar will be God's house, and of everything you give me I will give a tenth back to you."

Genesis 28:10-22

One time, after eating and drinking in Shiloh, Hannah got up and presented herself before the LORD. (Now Eli the priest was sitting in the chair by the doorpost of the LORD's temple.) Hannah was very upset and couldn't stop crying as she prayed to the LORD. Then she made this promise: "LORD of heavenly forces, just look at your servant's pain and remember me! Don't forget your servant! Give her a boy! Then I'll give him to the LORD for his entire life. No razor will ever touch his head."

As she kept praying before the LORD, Eli watched her mouth. Now Hannah was praying in her heart; her lips were moving, but her voice was silent, so Eli thought she was drunk.

"How long will you act like a drunk? Sober up!" Eli told her.

"No sir!" Hannah replied. "I'm just a very sad woman. I haven't had any wine or beer but have been pouring out my heart to the LORD. Don't think your servant is some good-for-nothing woman. This whole time I've been praying out of my great worry and trouble!"

Eli responded, "Then go in peace. And may the God of Israel give you what you've asked from him."

"Please think well of me, your servant," Hannah said. Then the woman went on her way, ate some food, and wasn't sad any longer.

They got up early the next morning and worshipped the Lord. Then they went back home to Ramah. Elkanah had sex with his wife Hannah, and the Lord remembered her. So in the course of time, Hannah conceived and gave birth to a son. She named him Samuel, which means "I asked the LORD for him." . . .

When [Samuel] had been weaned and was still very young, Hannah took him, along with a three-year-old bull, an ephah of flour, and a jar of wine, and brought him to the LORD's house at Shiloh. They slaughtered the bull, then brought the boy to Eli.

"Excuse me, sir!" Hannah said. "As surely as you live, sir, I am the woman who stood here next to you, praying to the LORD. I prayed for this boy, and the LORD gave me what I asked from him. So now I give this boy back to the LORD. As long as he lives, he is given to the LORD."

Then they worshipped there before the LORD.

1 Samuel 1:9-20, 24-28

Brothers and sisters, we want to let you know about the grace of God that was given to the churches of Macedonia. While they were being tested by many problems, their extra amount of happiness and their extreme poverty resulted in a surplus of rich generosity. I assure you that they gave what they could afford and even more than they could afford, and they did it voluntarily. They urgently begged us for the privilege of sharing in this service for the saints. They even exceeded our expectations, because they gave themselves to the Lord first and to us, consistent with God's will. As a result, we challenged Titus to finish this work of grace with you the way he had started it.

Be the best in this work of grace in the same way that you are the best in everything, such as faith, speech, knowledge, total commitment, and the love we inspired in you. I'm not giving an order, but by mentioning the commitment of others, I'm trying to prove the authenticity of your love also. You know the grace of our Lord Jesus Christ. Although he was rich, he became poor for your sakes, so that you could become rich through his poverty.

I'm giving you my opinion about this. It's to your advantage to do this, since you not only started to do it last year but you wanted to do it too. Now finish the job as well so that you finish it with as much enthusiasm as you started, given what you can afford. A gift is appreciated because of what a person can afford, not because of what that person can't afford, if it's apparent that it's done willingly. . . .

Everyone should give whatever they have decided in their heart. They shouldn't give with hesitation or because of pressure. God loves a cheerful giver. God has the power to provide you with more than enough of every kind of grace. That way, you will have everything you need always and in everything to provide more than enough for every kind of good work.

2 Corinthians 8:1-12; 9:7-8

Getting Started

Opening Activity

As participants gather, greet each one by name (and, if you choose, invite participants to fill out and wear a name tag). When all have arrived, make introductions as necessary and express your enthusiasm for this study of *The Passion Play*. Ask group members why they've chosen to take part in the study, and tell them why you are interested in and eager to lead it.

Lead participants in brainstorming a list of promises people make, writing down their responses. After gathering a long list of responses, ask if participants would classify any of these promises as "vows" and, if so, why. Ask: "What makes a vow different from other kinds of promises?"

Ask this question from *The Passion Play*: "How big a part have [vows] played in your story?" (page 14). Invite volunteers to briefly share stories of important vows in their lives (as

Rob Fuquay does at the beginning of chapter 1) or in their family histories.

Tell your group this session explores the power vows can have on our identity and our faith by reflecting on the people of Oberammergau's vow to stage a passion play.

Opening Prayer

> Ever-giving, ever-faithful God, thank you for this time we have to learn from the people of Oberammergau, from one another, from Holy Scripture, and from your Spirit. May we discover the commitments to which you call us and rediscover your constant commitment to us, for the sake of Jesus Christ, your Son, our Savior. Amen.

Video Discussion

Watch "The Vow" (*The Passion Play* DVD, Session 1). After the video, discuss:

- What interests or intrigues you most about the Oberammergau Passion Play tradition?
- In his book, Rob Fuquay writes, "Passion plays were popular throughout Europe and were a common way for a community to express its faith and devotion" (pages 15-16). Why do you think passion plays have proved so compelling throughout history?
- In the video, Fuquay points out the crucifix before which the people of Oberammergau made their vow to God. What does looking at this crucifix make you think or feel? Do crucifixes play a part in your worship, individually or with your congregation? Why or why not?
- How has the people's vow to stage a passion play every decade shaped the community of Oberammergau? How might you compare this vow's impact to the potential impact a vow to build a chapel or monument could have had?

Book Discussion

Ask participants who have read "The Power of a Vow" (*The Passion Play*, chapter 1) to talk briefly about what they found most interesting, or what questions the reading raised. Discuss:

- Have you ever made a vow to God? What were the circumstances that led to your vow? How seriously did you take the vow then? How seriously do you take it now? What has happened in your life because you kept or did not keep your vow?
- Rob Fuquay writes, "For many of us, we don't make God all we need until God is all we've got" (page 17). How much have you found this claim to be true in your own or others' experience?
- Fuquay notes the Oberammergau Passion Play vow troubles some people because it "feels like a bargain with God" (page 17). Is it ever acceptable to try to bargain with God? Why or why not? How do the Scriptures below help us think about bargaining with God?

    » Genesis 18:16-23—Abraham intercedes for the people of Sodom.
    » Exodus 32:7-14—Moses intercedes with God for the Israelites.
    » 2 Corinthians 12:7-10—Paul asks God to remove the "thorn in [his] body."

- Instead of viewing vows as bargains with God, Fuquay suggests, the people in Oberammergau are "promising what we will do in advance" with what God gives us (page 21). How do we distinguish between presumption of and trust in God's goodness?
- Fuquay notes the last plague victim in Oberammergau died in July 1633, but the traditional date of the town's vow is October 28. He suggests this delay means we often "recognize God's active hand [only]

with the perspective of time and distance" (page 22). When have time and distance allowed you to see what God has done in your past? How does this insight sustain your present faith in God, and give you hope for what God will do in your future?

- Fuquay distinguishes between vows and oaths: "Oaths typically involve affairs of this world. . . . Vows, on the other hand, involve God" (page 23). Do you find this distinction useful or significant? Why or why not?
- Fuquay says vows can give us a sense of purpose larger than ourselves: "What vows have you made that give you a reason to live?" (page 26). How would you respond?
- "God takes our vows and does more with them than we can know or sometimes foresee," Fuquay writes (page 27). What examples can you give of God using your or someone else's vow to do more good than the person who made the vow imagined?

Scripture Discussion

Form two groups of participants. Instruct one group to read Genesis 28:10-22; the other, 1 Samuel 1:9-20, 24-28. Have each group discuss these questions about its assigned passage (write these questions on the newsprint or marker board for ease of reference):

- Who is in trouble in this story, and why?
- What prompts the character in this story to make a vow to God?
- What does the character promise to God? What does the character want from God?
- What, if anything, does God promise to the character?
- How are the promises God and the characters make in these stories kept?

Optional: Encourage groups to consult the Bible commentaries and dictionaries you have provided for additional background information about their assigned passage.

After allowing time for discussion, have each group report on its assigned passage. Once both groups have reported, discuss both stories using some or all of these questions:

- How are the vows in these two stories alike and different? Do you respond more favorably to one vow than the other? Why?
- Based on their vows, how would you describe or characterize Jacob's and Hannah's faith? How, if at all, would you like your faith to be more like theirs?
- Rob Fuquay describes Hannah's and Jacob's vows as "declaration[s] of obedience. . . . They were simply promising to honor God in advance" (pages 19–20). Do you agree with this assessment? Why or why not?
- When, if ever, have you or someone you know of promised to honor God in advance with blessings God provides? What happened?

Recruit a volunteer to read aloud 2 Corinthians 8:1-12; 9:7-8 while the rest of the group reads along silently. Before the reading, tell participants Paul is discussing the contribution believers in Corinth will make to the offering he's collecting to benefit believers in Jerusalem. After the reading, ask:

- What qualities about the Macedonian churches' vow and the way they kept it does Paul hold up as a model for the Corinthians?
- Why is the attitude with which we make and keep our vows as important as the vows themselves?
- Commenting on this passage, Rob Fuquay writes: "The fact is, God doesn't loan to us. God gives freely. Our vows to God are responses to God's blessing, not prerequisites for receiving" (page 24). How does Paul teach the Corinthians this lesson?

- How has seeing other people fulfill their vows inspired you to make and keep vows of your own?
- How does your church community encourage members to make and keep vows to God?

Closing Activity

You will need index cards or scrap paper; plate or basket used in your congregation to collect offerings; small cardboard box; packing tape.

Read aloud from *The Passion Play*: "What are reasons you have to make vows to God? . . . Our vows are always responses to God's grace" (pages 24–25). Allow time for participants to reflect silently on Fuquay's question and comment. Distribute the cards or paper and encourage participants to write a personal vow to God. Tell them they will not be asked to read their vows aloud or show them to anyone else unless they wish to do so.

After allowing sufficient time, instruct participants to fold their vows and to sign the outside. Have them place the vows in the offering basket or plate. Lead this or a similar prayer:

> You give to us so freely, O God. Now to you we freely make these vows, thankful for what you have already done and anticipating what you will yet do. Strengthen us to honor our commitments, that we may grow as faithful followers of Jesus Christ, crucified and risen. Amen.

As participants watch, transfer the vows to the box and seal it with packing tape. Tell the group the box will be kept in your meeting space (or some other mutually agreed upon location) and will not be opened until Session 6.

Session 2

THE IMPORTANCE OF COMMUNITY

Session Goals

This session's readings, video, conversations, and activities will help participants:

- Identify various communities that have helped form their sense of self and shape their faith.
- Appreciate how the Passion Play creates and sustains a sense of community in Oberammergau.
- Describe qualities and actions that define a Christ-centered community.
- Discuss characteristics of Christian community found in several stories from Scripture.
- Celebrate one another as important members of their faith community or wider community.

Scriptural Foundation

During that time, Jesus went out to the mountain to pray, and he prayed to God all night long. At daybreak, he called together his disciples. He chose twelve of them whom he called apostles: Simon, whom he named Peter; his brother Andrew; James; John; Philip; Bartholomew; Matthew; Thomas; James the son of Alphaeus; Simon, who was called a zealot; Judas the son of James; and Judas Iscariot, who became a traitor.

Luke 6:12-16

When Barnabas, Paul, and the delegates were sent on their way, they went down to Antioch. They gathered the believers and delivered the letter. The people read it, delighted with its encouraging message. Judas and Silas were prophets, and they said many things that encouraged and strengthened the brothers and sisters. Judas and Silas stayed there awhile, then were sent back with a blessing of peace from the brothers and sisters to those who first sent them. Paul and Barnabas stayed in Antioch, where, together with many others, they taught and proclaimed the good news of the Lord's word.

Some time later, Paul said to Barnabas, "Let's go back and visit all the brothers and sisters in every city where we preached the Lord's word. Let's see how they are doing." Barnabas wanted to take John Mark with them. Paul insisted that they shouldn't take him along, since he had deserted them in Pamphylia and hadn't continued with them in their work. Their argument became so intense that they went their separate ways. Barnabas took Mark and sailed to Cyprus. Paul chose Silas and left, entrusted by the brothers and sisters to the Lord's grace. He traveled through Syria and Cilicia, strengthening the churches.

Acts 15:30-41

Before the Festival of Passover, Jesus knew that his time had come to leave this world and go to the Father. Having loved his own who were in the world, he loved them fully.

Jesus and his disciples were sharing the evening meal. The devil had already provoked Judas, Simon Iscariot's son, to betray Jesus. Jesus knew the Father had given everything into his hands and that he had come from God and was returning to God. So he got up from the table and took off his robes. Picking up a linen towel, he tied it around his waist. Then he poured water into a washbasin and began to wash the disciples' feet, drying them with the towel he was wearing. . . .

After he washed the disciples' feet, he put on his robes and returned to his place at the table. He said to them, "Do you know what I've done for you? You call me 'Teacher' and 'Lord,' and you speak correctly, because I am. If I, your Lord and teacher, have washed your feet, you too must wash each other's feet. I have given you an example: Just as I have done, you also must do. . . .

"I give you a new commandment: Love each other. Just as I have loved you, so you also must love each other. This is how everyone will know that you are my disciples, when you love each other."

John 13:1-5, 12-15, 34-35

Getting Started

Opening Activity

Welcome participants, especially any attending the study for the first time. Remind the group that the first session explored the importance of vows. Invite participants who attended the previous session to talk about any connections they made between what they learned or experienced and their daily life (spark this discussion with an example of your own).

Read aloud from *The Passion Play*: "Think back on the happiest moments in your life. How many of them involved other people? . . . Most of our cherished memories involve others" (page 31). Tell participants about a "cherished memory" of your own that involves other people, then invite them to talk about such memories of their own. *Optional:* Ask participants with smartphones how many of the pictures on their devices feature happy moments shared with other people.

Tell participants Session 2 explores how and why our experience of community is important, as well as how and why God places us in communities.

Opening Prayer

Loving God, from whom every family on earth takes its name: You declared at our creation that it was not good for us to be alone, and placed us in relationship with one another. May the community we experience during this time of study, reflection, and prayer move us to connect more deeply with one another and to invite ever-widening circles into fellowship with us, that we may fulfill the life of love for which you designed us, and which you exemplified for us in your Son, Jesus Christ. Amen.

Video Discussion

Watch "Community" (*The Passion Play* DVD, Session 2). After the video, discuss:

- What is significant about the fact that Oberammergau's residents, not professional actors from elsewhere, perform the Passion Play?
- In 1634, the first Oberammergau Passion Play took place on a stage built over the graves of the town's plague victims. How might this proximity of stage and cemetery illustrate the nature of Christian community?
- In the Oberammergau cemetery, visitors can often remember what roles the people buried there played in the Passion Play, and how often. What "role" in your life or your community do you most want people who visit your grave to remember you for playing?
- Why and how do the people Fuquay interviews who are not part of the Passion Play still feel connected to their community through the event? What do their insights suggest about how people in your church community can experience closer connections to one another through shared experiences?
- What community-building and -nurturing experiences does or could your church offer to the community beyond your own membership?

Book Discussion

Ask participants who have read "The Importance of Community" (*The Passion Play*, chapter 2) to talk briefly about what they found most interesting, or what questions the reading raised. Discuss:

- Fuquay writes, "The experience of genuine community is a sacred gift" (page 32). What do you consider the hallmarks of "genuine" community, and why? How easy or difficult do you find it to experience such community? What experiences, if any, do you think our society attempts to substitute for genuine community?
- "If the only challenges we accept in life are ones we can do alone," writes Fuquay, "we aren't living with a high enough bar" (page 34). Talk about a time you successfully rose to a challenge as part of a community.
- Fuquay argues relationships with other Christians are essential to knowing and believing in Jesus (pages 35–36). How much do you agree or disagree, and why? How would you respond to someone who told you, "I don't have to be part of a church to be a Christian"?
- "It's been said that where the Lord builds a house of prayer, the devil builds a chapel" (page 36). What does this saying mean? How would you rephrase it in your own words? What illustrations of it, from your own or another's experience, can you offer?
- Fuquay relates how, at one point in Oberammergau's history, "day after day of performing" in the Passion Play together helped heal divisions between "traditionalists and reformers" (page 38). What activities or projects does your congregation undertake together on a regular basis that have the power to heal divisions and restore relationships?

- Do you agree with the surveys Fuquay cites that say "incivility has risen to a crisis level in our country" (page 38)? Why or why not? If you agree, on what or whom do you place the blame? In what practical ways does or could your church respond to incivility in our society today?
- Speculating the apostle Paul wrote a letter in which he sought reconciliation with Mark, Fuquay asks readers if they have any "lost letters"—not "actual letters you have written but ones that need to be written" (page 41). Think about to whom you would or could write a "lost letter." Would it be a letter of apology? Of yearning? Of forgiveness? Of blessing? If you wish, talk about what your letter to this person would say, and why.
- "For all that is wrong with the church," Fuquay contends, ". . . there is still something about the church that when it gets it right is the hope of the world" (page 43). He identifies this "something" as the "willingness to love as Jesus loved" (page 45). When was a time, if ever, that you experienced that kind of love as part of a Christian community?

Scripture Discussion

Invite participants to turn to and read Luke 6:12-16. Discuss:

- As Fuquay notes, this story introduces a distinction between Jesus' many "disciples" and his twelve "apostles." The Greek word for "apostle" means one who is sent. Apostles, as Fuquay writes, "have been invited to represent Jesus and have said, 'You can count on me' " (page 35). How does Luke 9:1-6 give us a more detailed understanding of what Jesus sent out his apostles to do?
- When have you found yourself (formally or informally)

being sent out into the world to represent Jesus? What happened?

- Why did Jesus spend the night praying before he selected his apostles (verse 12)?
- What, if anything, do you already know about the twelve apostles Jesus chose? What can you discover about them using a Bible dictionary, concordance, or other reference tool?
- To what extent did Judas Iscariot, in betraying Jesus, also betray the community of the apostles? What might we learn from Jesus' choice of Judas as an apostle?
- Fuquay emphasizes the twelve apostles experienced the difficulties of living in a Christ-centered community. How do Luke 9:46-50 and 22:24-27 illustrate his point?
- What can we learn today from the apostles about both the difficulty and the value of remaining in Christian community?

Read Acts 15:30-41. Discuss:

- What characteristics of Christian community do you notice in this passage?
- What intentional efforts do the Christians in this story take to foster a Christ-centered community? How are these efforts like and unlike the things your congregation does?
- Why did Paul and Barnabas disagree over taking John Mark on their journey? How did they move past this disagreement? How is their resolution of this conflict instructive for Christian communities today?
- Based on 2 Timothy 4:11, Fuquay speculates that Paul eventually reconciled with Mark. When have you witnessed Christian communities helping people heal their broken relationships?

Read John 13:1-5, 12-15, 34-35. Discuss:

- In John's Gospel, the meal Jesus shares with his disciples before his arrest is not the Passover Seder, but simply "the evening meal" (verse 2). Where and how have you experienced a meal's ability to create and nourish community? (You might also wish to reread Fuquay's story about Tom Shipp being turned away from his host family's dinner table, pages 45–47).
- In first-century near Eastern cultures, hosts usually provided water for guests to wash their own feet or had servants wash guests' feet. How does Jesus' washing his disciples' feet demonstrate what Fuquay calls the "apostolic spirit" (verse 45) that defines Christian community?
- Fuquay writes, "Willingness to love as Jesus loved may just be the most important attribute for being an apostle" (verse 45). What does your congregation regularly do as a community to demonstrate its willingness to love as Jesus loved? What more do you think could your congregation be doing, and why?

Closing Activity

Remind participants of how the names of the Oberammergau Passion Play cast members are written on a large chalkboard (as described in *The Passion Play* on pages 32–34). Write each of your group participants' names on the marker board or large sheet of paper. Next to each name, write a word or phrase describing a "role" the named participant "plays" or a contribution she or he makes to the congregation or the wider community. If desired, encourage the group to applaud each participant, just as the residents of Oberammergau applaud each name written on the cast board—and be certain to write your own name, too, giving participants a chance to identify your role and applaud you!

Lead this or a similar prayer:

Lord Jesus, you have claimed each one of us as your own, and in so doing you make us belong not only to you but also to one another. By your Spirit, may we grow in our willingness to love as you love, that the world may recognize you in and through us, as our community does everything in your name to the glory of God. Amen.

Session 3

THE ROLE OF RITUAL

Session Goals

This session's readings, video, conversations, and activities will help participants:

- Appreciate the ritual nature of the Oberammergau Passion Play.
- Identify important rituals in our society and in the church.
- Describe how ritual's power has shaped their individual sense of identity and of belonging to a community.
- Examine biblical examples of ritual from both the Old and New Testaments.
- Consider the place and power of ritual in the life of their congregation.

Scriptural Foundation

The Lord said to Moses: Speak to the Israelites and say to them: These are my appointed times, the Lord's appointed times, which you will declare to be holy occasions: Work can be done for six days, but the seventh day is a Sabbath of special rest, a holy occasion. You must not do any work on it; wherever you live, it is a Sabbath to the Lord. . . .

> *Once you enter the land that I am giving you, the land must celebrate a sabbath rest to the* Lord. *You will plant your fields for six years, and prune your vineyards and gather their crops for six years. But in the seventh year the land will have a special sabbath rest, a Sabbath to the* Lord: *You must not plant your fields or prune your vineyards. You must not harvest the secondary growth of your produce or gather the grapes of your freely growing vines. It will be a year of special rest for the land. . . . Count off seven weeks of years—that is, seven times seven—so that the seven weeks of years totals forty-nine years. Then have the trumpet blown on the tenth day of the seventh month. Have the trumpet blown throughout your land on the Day of Reconciliation. You will make the fiftieth year holy, proclaiming freedom throughout the land to all its inhabitants. It will be a Jubilee year for you: each of you must return to your family property and to your extended family.*
>
> *Leviticus 23:1-3; 25:2-5, 8-10*

> *When the time came, Jesus took his place at the table, and the apostles joined him. He said to them, "I have earnestly desired to eat this Passover with you before I suffer. I tell you, I won't eat it until it is fulfilled in God's kingdom." After taking a cup and giving thanks, he said, "Take this and share it among yourselves. I tell you that from now on I won't drink from the fruit of the vine until God's kingdom has come." After taking the bread and giving thanks, he broke it and gave it to them, saying, "This is my body, which is given for you. Do this in remembrance of me." In the same way, he took the cup after the meal and said, "This cup is the new covenant by my blood, which is poured out for you."*
>
> *Luke 22:14-20*

Getting Started

Before Session 3, prepare several index cards by writing on each one:

- the name of a ritual with which your participants are likely familiar.

- five words or short phrases commonly associated with each ritual—use the first that come to your mind.

For example, three of your cards might read:

WEDDING	GRADUATION	BIRTHDAY PARTY
rings	diploma	cake
dress	processional	presents
bouquet	cap and gown	candles
bride	school	ice cream
groom	speeches	sing

Your group will use these cards in your session's Opening Activity.

Opening Activity

Welcome participants, especially any attending the study for the first time. Remind the group that the previous session explored the importance of community. Invite participants who attended to talk about any connections they made between what they learned and their experiences in various communities to which they belong during the week (spark this discussion with an example of your own).

Invite participants to take one index card from your stack of prepared cards—"face down," with the written on side hidden—and to play a game like "Taboo." Each participant has one minute (you will serve as timekeeper) to describe the ritual on the card they selected for the whole group, without using any of the words underneath the name of the ritual.

Tell participants Session 3 explores how and why rituals exert such a powerful influence on our sense of identity. Ask this question from *The Passion Play*: "What are rituals that make up your life?" (page 52). Allow a few minutes for participants to respond. Encourage them to name daily, weekly, yearly, and less-frequent rituals.

Opening Prayer

Eternal God, you have always commanded your people to observe rituals in order to grow in faith and glorify you. As we consider the place and power of ritual in our lives, help us also, by your Spirit, to discern the new ways you connect with and call to us through even the old and familiar practices that mark us as disciples of your Son, our Savior, Jesus Christ. Amen.

Video Discussion

Watch "Ritual" (*The Passion Play* DVD, Session 3). After the video, discuss:

- What rituals surround the Passion Play in Oberammergau beyond the every-decade performance itself? What impact do these rituals have on people's personal faith?
- As you watch the footage from the Last Supper scene in past Passion Plays, what do you think and feel? How does seeing this scene performed connect with your experiences of Holy Communion (the Lord's Supper)?
- Rob Fuquay highlights the table and props used in the Passion Play's Last Supper scene. How are they like or unlike the table (altar) and items used in your church's celebrations of Holy Communion? How important are the objects used in the Communion ritual? Why?

Book Discussion

Ask participants who have read "The Role of Ritual" (*The Passion Play*, chapter 3) to talk briefly about what they found most interesting, or what questions the reading raised. Discuss:

- "Rituals are the couplings that hold together our past and our future," Fuquay writes (page 53). What does he mean? Do you agree? Why or why not?

- Noting how much of the Oberammergau Passion Play's impact comes from its decennial frequency, Fuquay asks readers to reflect on "the unique power of having traditions or rituals that might get celebrated just a handful of times, or even just once, in your lifetime" (page 52). What are some of the "once in a lifetime" rituals you have experienced? How do you still feel those rituals' impact today?
- Fuquay cites Emory University research that reveals "families who practiced rituals, such as dinnertime conversations in which knowledge of their past was shared, helped to deepen children's identity" (page 54). What rituals, if any, in your family of origin or your current family communicated knowledge of your past to you? How did or do these rituals contribute to your sense of who you are?
- Fuquay writes, "Knowing people in our past who persevered through adversity gives us the hope that we can as well" (page 54). What stories of such people from your personal or family past do you know, and how have these stories helped you? How does Hebrews 11:1–12:2 serve this function for God's family of faith to which we belong?
- In discussing Holy Communion, Fuquay writes, "God understands that we all need regular routines and practices to stay connected to the Eternal" (page 57). What rituals around Communion—preparation, frequency, words spoken and sung, manner of distributing the bread and wine or juice, and so on—does your congregation observe? How do you experience their potential to connect you to God? What Communion rituals, if any, from other congregations and traditions have you seen or taken part in that you find powerful?

- What is the difference between a ritual and a habit? What are some good habits you're glad you've developed? How did you do so? What are some bad habits you'd like to break?
- "The ritual of active participation in a vital spiritual community," writes Fuquay, "helps us become our best selves" (page 59). Do you agree? Why or why not?
- Fuquay notes how religious or spiritual rituals can provide "solace in connecting us to the God who brings order out of chaos" (page 61). What rituals, if any, do you depend on to provide you such solace? When, if ever, have you been surprised to find solace in a religious or spiritual ritual?
- Fuquay writes that the people of Oberammergau have sometimes struggled with the temptation to make the Passion Play ritual—the scripts, the music—"sacrosanct," rather than remembering the sacred reality to which the ritual points (page 61). When has your congregation wrestled with this same kind of temptation? What happened? How can spiritual communities guard against this temptation before it becomes a problem?

Scripture Discussion

Have participants turn to and read Leviticus 23:1-3; 25:2-5, 8-10. (You will want to write the citation on the board or newsprint for ease of reference. Consider forming three groups of participants, assigning each group one of the sections to read and discuss.) Discuss:

- Fuquay points to the Sabbath as one way "ancient Jews understood the power of ritual" (page 52), and modern observant Jews continue to celebrate the Sabbath. What sets the Sabbath apart? While Leviticus 23 doesn't specify why the Sabbath is holy, what reasons for its holiness are given in Exodus 20:11 and Deuteronomy 5:15?

- Sunday is often called the Christian Sabbath or the Lord's Day because Jesus was raised from the dead on a Sunday. With what rituals do you observe the Christian Sabbath?
- To what extent is any given Sunday "a Sabbath of special rest, a holy occasion" (Leviticus 23:2) for you? What changes, if any, would you like to make to your Sabbath observance?
- How does Leviticus 25 connect the observance of Sabbath years to the well-being of the land? How does this ritual practice shape people's dependence upon God? What might a "Sabbath year" look like in our modern society?
- How does the Jubilee year—what Fuquay calls "sort of a Sabbath of Sabbath years" (page 52)—connect Sabbath observance with the well-being of the social order? What lessons can our modern society learn from the ritual practice of the Jubilee?
- How important do you think it is for the church to encourage observance of the Sabbath, and why? What practical forms does or could that encouragement take?

Have participants turn to and read Luke 22:14-20. Discuss:

- Fuquay points out the meal Jesus shared with his disciples in Luke was "not Holy Communion, but a Passover or Seder meal" (page 55). Participating in this ritual meal with his disciples helped prepare Jesus for "the pain and loneliness he was about to face." Why is it important to remember Jesus was devoutly observing Jewish ritual before his death?
- How do Jesus' words to and actions with his disciples at the table add new or additional meaning to the symbolism of the Passover ritual? When and how have

you experienced established and familiar rituals taking on new and additional levels of meaning?

- Some congregations hold "Christian Seders" in which the established Seder is interpreted, wholly or in part, with reference to Jesus. What do you think about this practice? What do you imagine or know a devout Jew would think about a "Christian Seder"?
- Fuquay writes Jesus knows his disciples "will need something to touch and hold as a reminder that God has a hold of them" (pages 56–57). What physical things and actions serve this purpose for you?

Closing Activity

Fuquay suggests "keeping a time capsule in which you renew and update the important vows of your life" (page 53) as an appropriate way to mark important but infrequent rituals. Invite participants to plan their personal time capsules. What physical objects would they place in them? What memories? And, as Fuquay suggests, what vows? Allow the group a few minutes to write their responses on scrap paper, then invite volunteers to share some of the contents of their time capsules.

Read aloud from *The Passion Play*: "We are in large part what we choose to remember" (page 54). Lead this or a similar prayer:

> O God, you are beyond all time, yet you have entered time to claim a people for yourself. May your Spirit always strengthen our remembrance that we belong to you, and may we live out our identity as your people in not only our rituals but also every action of our lives. We ask it in the name of Jesus Christ. Amen.

Session 4

LIVING THE STORY

Session Goals

This session's readings, video, conversations, and activities will help participants:

- Discuss the expectations placed on people who perform in the Oberammergau Passion Play.
- Identify the expectations of righteousness Christ holds for his disciples today.
- Consider how others have called forth the best in them, and how they might call forth the best in others in their daily living.

Scriptural Foundation

[Jesus said,] "Don't even begin to think that I have come to do away with the Law and the Prophets. I haven't come to do away with them but to fulfill them. I say to you very seriously that as long as heaven and earth exist, neither the smallest letter nor even the smallest stroke of a pen will be erased from the Law until everything there becomes a reality. Therefore, whoever ignores one of the least of these commands and teaches others to do the same will be called the lowest in the kingdom of heaven. But whoever keeps these

commands and teaches people to keep them will be called great in the kingdom of heaven. I say to you that unless your righteousness is greater than the righteousness of the legal experts and the Pharisees, you will never enter the kingdom of heaven. . . .

"Everybody who hears these words of mine and puts them into practice is like a wise builder who built a house on bedrock. The rain fell, the floods came, and the wind blew and beat against that house. It didn't fall because it was firmly set on bedrock. But everybody who hears these words of mine and doesn't put them into practice will be like a fool who built a house on sand. The rain fell, the floods came, and the wind blew and beat against that house. It fell and was completely destroyed."

Matthew 5:17-20; 7:24-27

Everything is permitted, but everything isn't beneficial. Everything is permitted, but everything doesn't build others up. No one should look out for their own advantage, but they should look out for each other. Eat everything that is sold in the marketplace, without asking questions about it because of your conscience. The earth and all that is in it belong to the Lord. *If an unbeliever invites you to eat with them and you want to go, eat whatever is served, without asking questions because of your conscience. But if someone says to you, "This meat was sacrificed in a temple," then don't eat it for the sake of the one who told you and for the sake of conscience. Now when I say "conscience" I don't mean yours but the other person's. Why should my freedom be judged by someone else's conscience? If I participate with gratitude, why should I be blamed for food I thank God for? So, whether you eat or drink or whatever you do, you should do it all for God's glory. Don't offend either Jews or Greeks, or God's church. This is the same thing that I do. I please everyone in everything I do. I don't look out for my own advantage, but I look out for many people so that they can be saved. Follow my example, just like I follow Christ's.*

1 Corinthians 10:23–11:1

Getting Started

Opening Activity

Welcome participants, especially any attending the study for the first time. Remind the group that the previous session explored the importance of ritual. Invite participants who attended to talk about any connections they made between what they learned and their experiences of various rituals—formal or informal, personal or communal—during the week (spark this discussion with an example of your own).

Brainstorm with participants a list of actors and their most famous roles. Now ask participants to identify which actors are (as far as they can know from media reports) notably like or unlike these characters. Ask: "How much of a congruity do you expect or want between an actor and his or her role? Why?"

Tell participants this session uses the expectations placed on the cast of the Oberammergau Passion Play as a springboard for talking about how we "act out" our Christian faith.

Opening Prayer

O God, you call your people to be holy as you are holy, and perfect as you are perfect. May your Spirit so guide our time of study and discussion today that we might better understand what it means to live as your righteous ones, enacting the story of the crucified and risen Christ every day. Amen.

Video Discussion

Watch "Living the Story" (*The Passion Play* DVD, Session 4). After the video, discuss:

- How does knowing the people who perform the Oberammergau Passion Play are not professional actors affect your response to it?
- What do you find most interesting about the firsthand accounts in the video of what it's like to perform in the Passion Play?

- How do you imagine seeing their friends and neighbors onstage in the Passion Play shapes the way residents of Oberammergau experience the story?
- Do you think the high expectations placed on the Passion Play performers are appropriate? Why or why not?
- Fuquay interviews an actor who has played Jesus in the play. To what extent does Jesus call all Christians to "play him" in life?
- What is the Pilatushaus, and why does Fuquay say it is significant? What insights into glorifying God through your daily work (whether paid or unpaid) does Fuquay's trip to the Pilatushaus give you?

Book Discussion

Ask participants who have read "Living the Story" (*The Passion Play*, chapter 4) to talk briefly about what they found most interesting, or what questions the reading raised. Discuss:

- Fuquay asserts, "The Passion Play gives meaning to everyone's life in Oberammergau" (page 67). What evidence supports his statement? What experiences in your community give meaning to everyone's life, whether or not everyone directly participates in them?
- If you were to act in a passion play, in what role would you want to be cast, and why? Is there any role you would definitely *not* want? Why?
- Fuquay compares the expectations placed, rightly or wrongly, on actors in the Oberammergau Passion Play to the expectations placed on Christians. Talk about a time you have encountered a non-Christian's expectations for Christians. Did you confirm or challenge those expectations? How?
- Fuquay quotes Cardinal Friedrich Wetter: "The person imitating Jesus doesn't act the part, he has to *be* Jesus. To act it is impossible" (page 68). What distinction

do you think the cardinal was making? How much do you agree with him?

- "Many congregations today," Fuquay notes, "struggle to keep their youth interested and involved in church" (page 69). Does your congregation face this challenge? If so, what are you doing to meet it? If not, how are you keeping youth and younger members active and engaged?
- Fuquay describes how many people in Oberammergau, such as Frederik Mayet, are "not apathetic toward faith" but feel "disappointment toward the church" (page 71). When, if ever, have you felt the church has let you down? How, if at all, did you handle that disappointment?
- "Certainly," Fuquay states, "Jesus did not intend to form an institution" (page 71). How much do you agree or disagree with this assertion, and why? If an institutional church was not Jesus' intention, is the institutional church Jesus' will for believers today?
- Fuquay draws a distinction between religion and righteousness (pages 71–72). What is this distinction, and do you agree with it? Why or why not?
- To what stories about Jesus would you point to illustrate Fuquay's statement that Jesus displayed "a higher righteousness" than religion in his own life (page 72)?
- According to Fuquay, "The power of the Passion story is not that there are clear lines of distinction between good and bad characters. We are meant to see ourselves in all of them" (page 73). Talk about a time when you were aware of the "mishmash of competing drives, ambitions, and desires" within yourself (page 75). What steps do you take to help you desire "to do good in spite of the bad" (page 75)? How is God involved in your inner wrestling between good and bad?
- "God usually sends messengers to call forth the angels

in us" (page 75). Who have been the messengers in your life who have called forth your inner angel, the "things in you that you didn't see in yourself" (page 76)? When, if ever, have you been such a messenger for someone else—or for whom might you be such a messenger now?

- Fuquay's discussion with one Oberammergau woodworker leads him to reflect on Martin Luther's doctrine of the priesthood of all believers: the idea that all Christians (not just ordained clergy) are called to minister. How and to whom do or could you minister in your daily life? What specific places can be, as Fuquay writes, "the stages in your life" where God can use you as "an influence of love and hope" (page 79)?

Scripture Discussion

Recruit two volunteers to "play Jesus" by reading aloud his words from the Sermon on the Mount. One volunteer will read Matthew 5:17-20; the other, Matthew 7:24-27. Encourage each volunteer to read with appropriate emphasis and emotion. If volunteers are unfamiliar or uncomfortable with reading Scripture in this way, remind them that every out-loud reading of Scripture is an interpretation of it, and it is better to read Scripture aloud carefully than carelessly.

After the first reading, thank your first "Jesus," then discuss:

- "The Law" (in Hebrew, *Torah*) and "the Prophets" (*Nevi'im*) are the first two divisions in the Tanakh, the Jewish Bible (the third is "the Writings," *Ketuvim*). How does Jesus define his relationship to Israel's past with God, as revealed and recorded in what Christians call the Old Testament?
- In what way does Jesus "fulfill" the Law and the Prophets?
- Commenting on this passage, Fuquay writes, "Righ-

teousness is about being rightly aligned with God. . . . [It] is about God's work to line up God's way of life in our lives, a way that comes into view in the life of Jesus" (page 72). How would you define "righteousness" for someone unfamiliar with the idea?

- If righteousness is God's work, how can Jesus demand a "higher righteousness" (page 72) from his followers?
- The commandments in the Law served to identify God's people as holy, or "set apart," for God's work in the world. Does or should the Law retain this function for Christians? How do Christians maintain their identity as belonging to God?
- Some other New Testament passages, especially in Paul's letters, could be read to suggest that Christians no longer need to observe the Law (for example, Galatians 2:15-21; Romans 7:1-6). Does this idea contradict what Jesus teaches in this passage? Why or why not?

After the second reading, thank your second "Jesus," then discuss:

- Fuquay says Jesus' parable "points out the distinction between *listening* and *living*" (page 69). What *is* that distinction? How do you understand the two different outcomes Jesus describes?
- How does Jesus' story help us understand the relationship between faith and action in living as his follower?

Have participants turn to and read 1 Corinthians 10:23–11:1. Discuss:

- In 1870, Joseph Daisenberger told the Oberammergau cast, "The eyes of many strangers will be fixed not only on the Play, but on ourselves" (page 68). How might the situation of the play cast be like the situation the apostle Paul addresses when writing to the Christians in Corinth?

- Buying meat that had not been sacrificed in non-Christian temples was difficult in ancient Roman society. How does Paul advise Christians to navigate this difficulty?
- What are some activities or situations today in which Christians face similar questions about whether to participate?
- When, if ever, have you limited your own freedom in Christ in order to avoid giving offense?
- How do we discern when Christian leaders are following Christ's example, as Paul says he does? Would or do you offer yourselves to others as a Christian role model? Why or why not?

Closing Activity

Read aloud from *The Passion Play*: "Whatever you do in your life can become a platform for God to use. . . . What are the stages in your life God can use to be an influence of love and hope in other people's lives?" (page 79). Close the session by inviting participants to reflect on Fuquay's question in silence for a minute or two. After the silence, invite any who wish to share their responses aloud.

Lead this or a similar prayer:

> You do not call us out of the world, O Christ, but send us into the world as your representatives. May we live out your words and your story ever more faithfully, that more people around us may know your grace and love. Amen.

Session 5

TELLING A BETTER STORY

Session Goals

This session's readings, video, conversations, and activities will help participants:

- Reflect on the importance of stories in shaping our sense of who we are and who other people are, especially those who are different from us.
- Identify anti-Semitic interpretations of the passion story.
- Understand how past productions of the Oberammergau Passion Play perpetuated anti-Semitic attitudes and beliefs, and how recent changes to the play seek to avoid perpetuating them.
- Through reading and discussing the "parable of the Good Samaritan," appreciate Jesus' use of fictional stories to challenge harmful social "narratives" in his time.
- Practice "rewriting the script" of an incident from

their own life or from current events in order to "tell a better story."

Scriptural Foundation

I'm speaking the truth in Christ—I'm not lying, as my conscience assures me with the Holy Spirit: I have great sadness and constant pain in my heart. I wish I could be cursed, cut off from Christ if it helped my brothers and sisters, who are my flesh-and-blood relatives. They are Israelites. The adoption as God's children, the glory, the covenants, the giving of the Law, the worship, and the promises belong to them. The Jewish ancestors are theirs, and the Christ descended from those ancestors. He is the one who rules over all things, who is God, and who is blessed forever. Amen.

But it's not as though God's word has failed. Not all who are descended from Israel are part of Israel. Not all of Abraham's children are called Abraham's descendants, but instead your descendants will be named through Isaac. That means it isn't the natural children who are God's children, but it is the children from the promise who are counted as descendants. . . .

I don't want you to be unaware of this secret, brothers and sisters. That way you won't think too highly of yourselves. A part of Israel has become resistant until the full number of the Gentiles comes in. In this way, all Israel will be saved, as it is written:

The deliverer will come from Zion.
He will remove ungodly behavior from Jacob.
This is my covenant with them,
when I take away their sins.

According to the gospel, they are enemies for your sake, but according to God's choice, they are loved for the sake of their ancestors. God's gifts and calling can't be taken back. Once you were disobedient to God, but now you have mercy because they were disobedient. In the same way, they have also been disobedient because of the mercy that you received, so now they can receive mercy too. God has locked up all people in disobedience, in order to have mercy on all of them.

God's riches, wisdom, and knowledge are so deep! They are as mysterious as his judgments, and they are as hard to track as his paths!

Who has known the Lord's mind?
Or who has been his mentor?
Or who has given him a gift
and has been paid back by him?
All things are from him and through him and for him.
May the glory be to him forever. Amen.

Romans 9:1-8; 11:25-36

A legal expert stood up to test Jesus. "Teacher," he said, "what must I do to gain eternal life?"

Jesus replied, "What is written in the Law? How do you interpret it?"

He responded, "You must love the Lord your God with all your heart, with all your being, with all your strength, and with all your mind, and love your neighbor as yourself."

Jesus said to him, "You have answered correctly. Do this and you will live."

But the legal expert wanted to prove that he was right, so he said to Jesus, "And who is my neighbor?"

Jesus replied, "A man went down from Jerusalem to Jericho. He encountered thieves, who stripped him naked, beat him up, and left him near death. Now it just so happened that a priest was also going down the same road. When he saw the injured man, he crossed over to the other side of the road and went on his way. Likewise, a Levite came by that spot, saw the injured man, and crossed over to the other side of the road and went on his way. A Samaritan, who was on a journey, came to where the man was. But when he saw him, he was moved with compassion. The Samaritan went to him and bandaged his wounds, tending them with oil and wine. Then he placed the wounded man on his own donkey, took him to an inn, and took care of him. The next day, he took two full days' worth of wages and gave them to the innkeeper. He said, 'Take care of him, and when I return, I will pay you back for any additional costs.' What do you think? Which one of these three was a neighbor to the man who encountered thieves?"

Then the legal expert said, "The one who demonstrated mercy toward him."

Luke 10:25-37

Getting Started

Opening Activity

Welcome participants, especially any attending the study for the first time. Remind the group that the previous session explored what it means to live out the story of Jesus' love in our daily lives. Invite participants who attended to talk about whether and how that session's discussions influenced their actions and attitudes in between sessions (be prepared to start this discussion by talking about your own experience).

Ask participants what their favorite story was when they were children. Was it a fable or fairy tale? A Bible story? A story from their family history? Encourage participants to identify why the story appealed to them, and what lessons about life, if any, they believe the story taught them. Be prepared to answer these questions regarding your own favorite childhood story.

Suggest that stories have a unique power to shape our sense of who we are and who others are, for good or for ill. Explain that this session explores how the Oberammergau Passion Play's telling of the story of Jesus' suffering and death has perpetuated dangerous anti-Semitic beliefs in the past, and how recent changes to the play attempt to tell the story in a better way.

Opening Prayer

God Most High, Holy One of Israel and Ruler of the Universe: You chose the family of Abraham and Sarah for salvation and service, and through Jesus you have mercifully joined us to your people.

Through our reading and reflection today, may your Spirit grant us greater awareness of what belonging to your people means for how we think about, talk about, and treat those who are different. Show us how to tell the story of your Son's passion so all people may hear it as good news. Amen.

Video Discussion

Watch "Living a Better Story" (*The Passion Play* DVD, Session 5). After the video, discuss:

- Why does Fuquay begin this session with a visit to the National Socialist Museum in Munich? How would you explain the museum's importance?
- What elements in the Oberammergau Passion Play made it something Hitler and the Nazi regime wanted to appropriate?
- According to the director and actor Fuquay talks with, how and why has the play's depiction of Judas shifted over time?
- What other changes have been made to the Passion Play to reframe or remove its anti-Semitic elements? What other changes have been made to the play in recent years to ensure it tells a better story?
- Do you think any of these changes described in this video substantially change the story of Jesus' passion? Why or why not?

Book Discussion

Ask participants who have read "Telling a Better Story" (*The Passion Play*, chapter 5) to talk briefly about what they found most interesting, or what questions the reading raised. Discuss:

- Adolf Hitler said the Oberammergau Passion Play was a convincing portrayal of "the menace of Jewry" and "the whole muck and mire of Jewry" (page 85). When have you seen or personally encountered, in overt or in subtle forms, this same anti-Semitic stereotype of the "dirty" and menacing, even evil, Jew?

- What are some reasons you think this stereotype has persisted throughout history? How do you respond when you hear or see instances of it?
- Fuquay calls Matthew 27:24-25 the "most offensive and inflammatory line in the passion narrative" (page 86). Why? How, if ever, have you heard preachers and teachers interpret these verses? How much do they affect your understanding of Jesus' passion? What relevance do these verses have for readers today?
- Fuquay cites *Nostra Aetate* (1965), the document in which the Second Vatican Council "repudiates all forms of anti-Semitism, particularly the charge that provokes so much of the hatred toward Jews: deicide" (page 85). That document reads, in part: "what happened in [Jesus'] passion cannot be charged against all the Jews, without distinction, then alive, nor against the Jews of today. Although the Church is the new people of God, the Jews should not be presented as rejected or accursed by God, as if this followed from the Holy Scriptures." Have you ever encountered one or both of these repudiated teachings? Why have these repudiated teachings proved so dangerous to Jews throughout history?
- Discussing the persistence of anti-Jewish beliefs, Fuquay mentions the "despicable attacks" Martin Luther, widely hailed as the "father" of the Protestant Reformation, wrote against Jews (page 87). Were you aware of Luther's anti-Jewish writings before reading this chapter? How, if at all, does knowing about them affect your view of or feelings about Luther?
- Fuquay writes about ways the Oberammergau Passion Play has been changed to present "Jesus as an observant Jew his whole life" (page 89). Why is it

important for non-Jews to remember Jesus was a Jew? How and how often does your congregation consider Jesus' Jewishness in worship, in Christian education, or in other settings?

- "Prejudice often prospers from false narratives that get passed down" (page 87). What other prejudices are you aware of, from your own or others' experience, that support Fuquay's statement?
- "Jesus was a master at telling stories that challenged the popular narratives of his day" (page 90). In addition to the "parable of the Good Samaritan," which Fuquay discusses at length, what other stories can you think of that Jesus told? How did these stories challenge prejudices and other preconceived ideas?
- Why do stories have a power to make us question our assumptions and even change our minds in ways that other kinds of communication—logical argument, emotional appeals, and so on—don't always have?
- Talk about a time a new story, or a story you heard in a new way, caused you to change your thoughts and/or your behavior.
- How is telling a different and better "story" about others and the world an act of "courage and faith" (page 96)? How can it lead to hope for the present and the future?

Scripture Discussion

Recruit a volunteer to read aloud Romans 9:1-8 and another to read aloud 11:25-36. Preface the readings by telling participants they are about to hear only the beginning and the ending of Paul's long, complicated discussion in Romans of why not all his fellow Jews have believed in Jesus as Messiah. After the readings, discuss:

- Why is Paul so distressed by many of his fellow Jews' lack of belief in Jesus (9:1-5)? What do his words suggest about how Christians should regard the Jewish background of their faith?

- How does Paul attempt to resolve the theological problem he sees in his fellow Jews' lack of faith in Jesus? How convincing do you find his reasoning?
- What does Paul say about Israel's ultimate destiny with God?
- Do you think Paul teaches faith in Christ supersedes, or replaces, Jewish faith in God? Why or why not?
- How does Paul attempt to keep his Gentile (non-Jewish) readers from thinking too highly of themselves (11:25, 33-36)? How can and do Christians share their faith in Jesus with a spirit of humility?
- Do you think Christians should evangelize Jews? If so, in what ways? If not, why not?

Recruit volunteers to read aloud Luke 10:25-37, reading these roles: the narrator, the legal expert, Jesus, and the Samaritan. Discuss:

- Fuquay claims anyone "at all familiar with this thing called church" is likely aware of "the historical origins of the Jewish-Samaritan divide" (page 92). What can you glean from Luke 9:51-55 (see *The Passion Play*, page 92) and John 4:1-10, 19-21 about this divide? What can you learn from a trusted Bible commentary or dictionary?
- Fuquay writes that with this parable, Jesus "took what was real: prejudice, religious intolerance, and false narratives and made up a better story" (page 92). How is Jesus' story better than the story that prevailed between Jews and Samaritans in his day?
- "Could it be," Fuquay asks, "that Jesus used fiction in the hope of changing reality?" (page 93). Has a fictional story ever prompted you to try to change the real world, or something in your real life? How? What happened?

- If you were to try to "make up a better story" about prejudice and intolerance among people today, whom would you cast as the "good Samaritan" in your parable, and why?

Closing Activity

You may need recent newspapers and magazines, or members' digital devices.

Read aloud from *The Passion Play*: "When we see perpetrators and idiots and rednecks and jerks as people, our narratives about them change, and so do our actions" (page 94).

Invite participants to think about an incident from their own lives, or from current events, in which they think of someone else as being "in the wrong," even if that "wrong" is only being different. You may wish to distribute recent newspapers and magazines to spark people's thinking, or invite members with digital devices to use them to review recent news headlines. Encourage participants to follow Fuquay's suggestion: "Take a bad incident that infuriates and inflames us and rewrite the script. Imagine the other person not as an evil culprit but a child of God" (page 96). Allow participants a few minutes to think about and write down some notes about a different, better narrative they could tell. Invite any volunteers (including, perhaps, yourself) to share responses, urging group members to respect one another's privacy after the session ends.

Lead this or a similar prayer:

> God of endlessly surprising imagination, ignite our hearts and minds that we may tell new stories and craft new narratives that include all people in present experiences of your loving grace, and envision places for them all in the redeemed, re-dreamed world you have promised to bring into being. Amen.

Session 6

THE POWER OF THE CROSS

Session Goals

This session's readings, video, conversations, and activities will help participants:

- Discuss the power of symbols in modern society and in the church.
- Understand the nature of crucifixion in the Roman Empire.
- Explore the meaning and significance of Jesus' cross.
- Compare and contrast several New Testament passages' interpretations of Jesus' death.
- Articulate their own understanding of what Jesus' cross means and why it matters.
- Reflect on their experience of making a keeping a vow to God during the course of this study.

Scriptural Foundation

From that time Jesus began to show his disciples that he had to go to Jerusalem and suffer many things from the elders, chief priests, and legal experts, and that he had to be killed and raised on the third day. Then Peter took hold of Jesus and, scolding him, began to correct him: "God forbid, Lord! This won't happen to you." But he turned to Peter and said, "Get behind me, Satan. You are a stone that could make me stumble, for you are not thinking God's thoughts but human thoughts."

Then Jesus said to his disciples, "All who want to come after me must say no to themselves, take up their cross, and follow me. All who want to save their lives will lose them. But all who lose their lives because of me will find them. Why would people gain the whole world but lose their lives? What will people give in exchange for their lives?"

Matthew 16:21-26

While we were still weak, at the right moment, Christ died for ungodly people. It isn't often that someone will die for a righteous person, though maybe someone might dare to die for a good person. But God shows his love for us, because while we were still sinners Christ died for us. So, now that we have been made righteous by his blood, we can be even more certain that we will be saved from God's wrath through him. If we were reconciled to God through the death of his Son while we were still enemies, now that we have been reconciled, how much more certain is it that we will be saved by his life? And not only that: we even take pride in God through our Lord Jesus Christ, the one through whom we now have a restored relationship with God.

Romans 5:6-11

There is one God and one mediator between God and humanity, the human Christ Jesus, who gave himself as a payment to set all people free. This was a testimony that was given at the right time.

1 Timothy 2:5-6

Dear friends, let's love each other, because love is from God, and everyone who loves is born from God and knows God. The person who doesn't love does not know God, because God is love. This is how the love of God is revealed to us: God has sent his only Son into the world so that we can live through him. This is love: it is not that we loved God but that he loved us and sent his Son as the sacrifice that deals with our sins.

Dear friends, if God loved us this way, we also ought to love each other.

1 John 4:7-11

Getting Started

Opening Activity

Welcome participants, especially any attending the study for the first time. Remind the group that the previous session explored the importance of "telling better stories" about people who are different from ourselves. Invite participants who attended to talk about whether and how the previous session helped them challenge any prejudicial ideas and actions they encountered in between sessions, particularly any anti-Semitic ones (be prepared to start this discussion by talking about your own experience).

Brainstorm with participants a list of readily identifiable non-religious symbols in modern society. (*Optional:* Before the session, gather images of such symbols—flags, monuments, sports team logos, etc.—and display them around your meeting space.) Once your group has completed its list, poll participants on which of these symbols they feel most strongly about (positively or negatively), and why. Discuss:

- What *makes* a symbol a symbol?
- What can cause symbols' meaning to change?
- How, if at all, are religious symbols different from other symbols?

Tell participants this final session explores the significance of the cross as a major Christian symbol, not only in Oberammergau but for believers everywhere.

Opening Prayer

God of majesty and mystery, whose glory none may see and live: By grace, we behold your glory in our Savior Jesus Christ, who gave himself on the cross to show forth your love. Guide our study and discussion today by your Spirit, that we may more and more become living symbols and bearers of your presence to each other and to the world. Amen.

Video Discussion

Watch "The Power of the Cross" (*The Passion Play* DVD, Session 6). After the video, discuss:

- According to Fuquay, why does the cross appear on many Alpine peaks? How is the prevalence of the cross in Alpine culture like or unlike its prevalence in ours?
- Which images of the cross from past Passion Plays particularly strike you as powerful, and why?
- How does Fuquay describe the difference between Roman Catholic and Protestant crosses? How, if at all, do you think these two kinds of crosses can complement each other?
- In the Oberammergau cemetery, Fuquay talks about how the Passion Play emerged from the village's great suffering. When have you been aware of something valuable coming out of your own or others' suffering?
- Fuquay talks with a parent who wants to share the Passion Play tradition with the next generation. What traditions do you most hope your faith community will pass on to its young people? What do you personally most want to leave as a legacy to the next generation of believers? Why?

Book Discussion

Ask participants who have read "The Power of the Cross" (*The Passion Play*, chapter 6) to talk briefly about what they found most interesting, or what questions the reading raised.

Discuss:

- Read the quote from nineteenth-century British explorer and traveler Sir Richard Burton at the start of this chapter (page 101). How valuable do you think "a live crucifix" is or can be to Christians? Have you ever found it valuable? Why?
- "Putting a cross on a [mountain] summit was a way to broadcast faith" (page 101). How do Christians in our culture "broadcast faith"? Do you think some ways are more appropriate or helpful than others? Which ones, and why?
- Fuquay notes the cross has not always been the primary symbol of Christian faith. He mentions "the dove, ship, anchor, lyre, and especially fish" as others (pages 102–103). How many, if any, of these ancient symbols are present in your church building, and where? What additional symbols of Christian faith other than the cross are prominent in your building? What do each of these symbols represent, specifically? (For example, the dove often represents the Holy Spirit.)
- Does your congregation have any symbols of faith particular to it—things that may not mean much to other Christians but which, for some reason, have great significance to you? If so, what are they, and how did they come to be powerful symbols for you?
- Historically speaking, why is the cross a surprising symbol for "love, grace, and mercy" (page 103)?
- Fuquay asks, "Can you think of ways today people use the cross as a sort of good-luck charm?" (page 105). What about other uses of the cross you think irreverent or inappropriate? How do you respond to such uses of the cross?
- Read Fuquay's description of the physical process of crucifixion (pages 105–106). Historical evidence provides these details; the Gospels do not. Why do you

think the Evangelists don't describe Jesus' physical death itself in such detail?

- Discussing the lack of a "single accepted theory" of the atonement, Fuquay writes "many Christians believe that the cross represents God's power and desire to take away all the damage and costs created by human sin and absorb the loss himself" (page 111). What language or images do you use to think about why Christ died and what his death accomplished?
- Fuquay writes "there is a place and need for both" plain crosses and crucifixes in Christian worship today (page 112). Do you agree? Why or why not?
- Fuquay wonders whether crucifixes began appearing to correct the association of the cross "with victory and success" that followed Emperor Constantine's adoption of Christianity (page 112). How else do or should Christians today focus on the humble, sacrificial, suffering love Jesus calls us to emulate?

Scripture Discussion

Recruit three volunteers to read aloud Matthew 16:21-26 (taking the roles of Jesus, Peter, and narrator). After the reading, discuss:

- What is "that time" (verse 21) from which Jesus begins to teach about his death and resurrection (see 16:13-20)? How does Jesus' prediction of his passion interpret what calling him "the Christ, the Son of the Living God" means (16:16)?
- Why does Jesus address Peter as "Satan" (verse 23)? How do you imagine Peter reacted to Jesus' rebuke?
- Commenting on this story, Fuquay writes that taking up a cross is not "being inconvenienced" or "fulfilling a chosen obligation" (page 106). Rather, "Jesus was inviting his followers to endure shame and humiliation" (page 107). Have you ever experienced "shame

and humiliation" because of your faith? Have you seen or known about others who have? What happened?

- Fuquay asks, "Can you think of any modern examples where people bring an expectation that their Christian faith should provide them victorious living while sparing them from suffering?" (page 105).
- To what "undesirable places" (page 107) has God called you to follow Jesus in the past? To what "humiliating places" (page 108) might God be calling you now?
- How do we discern and distinguish faithfully taking up one's cross from unhealthy and abusive situations we or others need to avoid for our own wholeness?

Read aloud from *The Passion Play* (page 110): "Different theories of the atonement present Jesus as a substitution for our sacrifice, a ransom paid to the devil, and a moral example or influence." All these theories find support in the New Testament.

Recruit three volunteers, each to read aloud one of the following Scriptures: Romans 5:6-11; 1 Timothy 2:5-6; 1 John 4:7-11. After each reading, ask participants:

- What dominant image(s) does this Scripture use to explain or explore the meaning of Christ's death?
- Does this Scripture fall neatly into one of the categories of atonement theories Fuquay mentions? Why or why not?
- What questions about Christ's death does this Scripture answer? What questions does it leave unanswered?

After all three readings, discuss:

- None of these Scriptures is an exercise in abstract theology. Each one addresses a problem or pastoral need early Christians faced. Looking at each Scripture in its immediate context, why does its author describe Christ's death as he does?

- What is the significance of the fact that the New Testament does not present one single theory of the atonement?

Closing Activity

Optional: Acquire and display a crucifix in your meeting space for this session, and/or obtain a small, inexpensive crucifix to give each participant (check with local religious supply stores or online retailers).

Read aloud from *The Passion Play* (page 114): "From beginning to end, the Bible declares that suffering is not contrary to faith but a part of it, and this truth is symbolized in the cross." Discuss:

- When, if ever, have you experienced suffering through which you believe God was working for good?
- How do or could such experiences of suffering help us grow as Christians?

Lead this or a similar prayer:

> Lord Jesus Christ, you promised that when you were lifted up, you would bring all things to yourself. We praise you for the love that led you to your cross, and from which nothing in all creation, not even death, can separate us. Send us forth as your cross-bearing people, empowered by your Spirit to love the world with the self-giving sacrificial passion with which you first loved us. Amen.

Before participants leave, retrieve the box of their written, folded, and signed vows you sealed and set aside at the end of Session 1. Open the box and allow participants to remove their vows. Invite volunteers to talk about whether and how they kept the vow they made when your group study began.

Express your hope that this study of Oberammergau's Passion Play will inspire all participants to experience the power of making and keeping promises to God, and thank group members for their participation in it. Exchange words of peace with one another as you depart.

CPSIA information can be obtained
at www.ICGtesting.com
Printed in the USA
LVHW030258140819
627542LV00004B/4

9 781501 884504